T0016387

US $9.99

£7.99

Gin Cocktails

From the Martini to the Negroni
The most popular Gin Recipes

Steve Quirk

NEW HOLLAND

Introduction

This book has been designed for the purpose of providing an extensive range of Gin-based cocktails from basic mixers through to exotic creations, demonstrating that there is nothing complicated about preparing and constructing a cocktail or mixed drink as you will discover after selecting cocktails to create from this book.

Each recipe is provided with clear and uncomplicated directions, ensuring that anybody who has never had the experience of creating a cocktail will be able to do so with ease.

Approximate % alcohol volume (% alc/vol) content has been calculated and supplied for each drink in this book, as well as how many standard drinks each contains.

These calculations are based on information obtained that is believed to be accurate and reliable, although cannot be guaranteed due to % alc/vol variations between the different brands of spirits and liqueurs. These calculations should only be used as a guide.

The % alc/vol for all spirits and liqueurs required for drinks contained within this book are provided in the glossary – if unsure then compare your spirits and liqueurs with the % alc/vol provided in the glossary.

Cocktails are what ?

The cocktail's origin is unknown, although there are many theories of how the word originated. One such theory is that during the American Revolution, in Betsy's Tavern, a French man toasted "vive le cocktail" after sighting bottles or glasses decorated with bird feathers by bartender Betsy Flanagan. Another theory is that the word originated from the practice of docking a horse's tail (cocktail) for mixed breeds as opposed to thoroughbreds, although I fail to see the connection between a horse's tail and a drink.

A more appropriate definition of a cocktail is a drink containing two or more ingredients served in glasses of various shapes and sizes. They are shaken, stirred, built, layered or blended.

Constructing a Cocktail

Shaking – When ingredients are required to be shaken, half fill a cocktail shaker with ice, and then pour ingredients into shaker over the ice. This will chill the ingredients quicker than pouring the ingredients into shaker before ice. Avoid over-filling your shaker – leave room for shaking.

To shake, stand still and shake vigorously for about ten seconds, strain into chosen glass and serve or garnish. The majority of cocktail shakers have a strainer; if yours does not then you can use a hawthorn strainer. Effervescent drinks should never be shaken in a cocktail shaker. Rinse shaker out thoroughly after each use and dry with a clean lint-free cloth. This will ensure that your drinks only have in them what they are supposed to and will not distort the flavour of the next drink that you prepare.

Stirring – Where ingredients are required to be stirred, half fill a mixing glass with ice and pour the ingredients over the ice. Stir and strain into chosen glass. Usually ingredients that mix easily together are prepared in this manner.

Building – To build a drink is to pour ingredients in order given into a highball glass over ice and serve with a swizzle stick for the recipient to admire and stir.

Layering – To layer a drink is to pour ingredients in order given (pour over the back of a spoon into chosen glass). This will allow the liquid to flow down the inside rim of glass, creating a layering effect. Usually the heavier ingredients are poured first.

Blending – When a blender is required, only use cracked or crushed ice in suitable blenders and blend until ingredients are evenly mixed.

Cocktails should be drunk as soon as they are served.

Useful Tips

Frosting – This is for the purpose of coating the rim of a glass with salt or sugar. This is achieved by moistening the rim of a glass using a slice of lemon or orange.

Then hold the chosen glass by its base or stem upside down and rest gently on a flat plate containing salt or caster sugar and twist slightly.

If you press down on glass too hard, this may result in chunks of salt or sugar sticking to rim. Lemon is used for salt-frosted rims and orange for sugar-frosted rims unless otherwise stated.

Sugar syrup – To make sugar syrup bring one cup of ordinary white sugar with one cup of water almost to the boil in a small saucepan stirring continuously and simmer until sugar is completely dissolved. Then remove from heat and allow to cool.

Once cool, pour into a re-sealable container or a corked bottle and store in refrigerator or behind your bar for regular use. This syrup will now last indefinitely.

Sweet and sour mix – To make sweet and sour mix bring one cup of sugar syrup to the simmer then add ½ cup fresh lemon juice and ½ cup fresh lime juice. Simmer till well mixed stirring frequently, then remove from heat and allow to cool.

Once cool, pour into a re-sealable container or corked bottle and store in refrigerator for upto one to two weeks. Sweet and sour mix is also refered to as sour mix or bar mix.

To chill a glass – Glasses can be chilled by placing them into a refrigerator or by placing ice cubes into the glasses while drinks are being prepared. Discard these ice cubes before pouring unless otherwise instructed.

To frost a glass – Where ingredients are required to be poured into a frosted glass, these glasses can be frosted by placing them into a freezer prior to use.

Fruit, peels and juices – Fruit slices and pieces will keep fresher and longer if covered with a damp clean linen cloth and refrigerated. Where citrus peel is required, cut the peel into required sizes and shave away the white membrane. Fruit and peels should be the last added ingredient to a cocktail (garnish). When juices are required remember – fresh is best. When using canned fruit and/or juices, transfer the can's contents into appropriate re-sealable containers and refrigerate.

Ice – It is important to maintain a well-stocked clean ice supply, as most cocktails require ice during construction. To obtain crushed ice if you do not have access to an ice-crushing machine, place required ice onto a clean linen cloth and fold up.

Place ice-filled cloth onto a hard surface and smash with a mallet - (not a bottle).

Large blocks of ice are often required for punches. These ice blocks can be made easily by using 2ltr and/or 4ltr empty ice-cream containers.

Measures

1 Dash	1ml (1/30fl oz)
1 Teaspoon	5ml (1/6fl oz)
1 Tablespoon	18ml (3/5fl oz)
1 Cup	250ml (8⅓fl oz)
1 Nip	30ml (1fl oz)

Gin

Gin originated from Holland in the seventeenth century when a Dutch physician produced Gin using juniper berries and alcohol for medicinal purposes.

Today Gin is produced by distilling grain mash such as barley, corn and rye in column stills.

This neutral spirit is then combined with water to reduce the strength before being redistilled with botanicals and aromatics.

The botanicals and aromatics required for this procedure are primarily juniper berries and coriander. Other botanicals and aromatics that are used by distillers include bitter almonds, caraway seeds, cinnamon, fennel, ginger, lemon and orange peel, roots and other secret ingredients.

Gin is an un-aged spirit with London Dry Gin being the most common type of Gin and is produced by distillers around the world. Dry Gin has become the preferred Gin consumed across the world with Dry Gin containing no sugar.

Genever or Hollands Gin is produced in pot stills containing a larger proportion of barley and other grains. This Gin is then redistilled with juniper berries.

Old Tom Gin is produced in England and is a sweet Gin.

Plymouth Gin is only produced in Plymouth, England and is a very Dry Gin.

Each distillery has their own formulas and processes for distilling and producing Gin, which is the most widely required spirit for cocktails.

Blues Martini

36.6% alc/vol
0.9 standard drinks

15 ml (½ fl oz) dry gin
15 ml (½ fl oz) vodka
dash blue curaçao

Pour ingredients into a mixing glass over ice and stir gently.

Strain into a martini glass over a small amount of cracked ice and serve.

Burnt Martini

38% alc/vol

2.7 standard drinks

60 ml (2 fl oz) dry gin

30 ml (1 fl oz) blended whiskey

Pour ingredients into a martini glass without ice and stir gently then serve.

Hawaiian Martini

31.4% alc/vol
2.2 standard drinks

60 ml (2 fl oz) dry gin
15 ml (½ fl oz) Cointreau
15 ml (½ fl oz) pineapple juice

Pour ingredients into a cocktail shaker over ice and shake.

Strain into a chilled martini glass and serve.

Dick Deming Martini

32% alc/vol
1.9 standard drinks

60 ml (2 fl oz) gin
15 ml (½ fl oz) white wine

Pour ingredients into a mixing glass over ice
and stir gently.

Strain into a chilled martini glass and serve.

Delmonico

28% alc/vol

1.5 standard drinks

23ml (¾fl oz) Dry Gin

15ml (½fl oz) Brandy

15ml (½fl oz) Dry Vermouth

15ml (½fl oz) Sweet
Vermouth

Twist of Lemon Peel

Pour the Gin, Brandy and Vermouths into a
mixing glass over ice.

Stir and strain into a chilled cocktail glass.

Add lemon peel and serve.

Gin Sling

12.2% alc/vol
1.7 standard drinks

60ml (2fl oz) Gin
Dash Grenadine
30ml (1fl oz) Fresh Orange Juice
90ml (3fl oz) Soda Water
Maraschino Cherry
Slice of Lemon

Pour Gin, Grenadine and juice into a highball glass over ice.

Add soda and stir gently.

Garnish with a cherry and slice of lemon then serve.

Gin Toddy

30.4% alc/vol
1.8 standard drinks

60ml (2fl oz) Dry Gin
10ml (⅓fl oz) Spring Water
½ teaspoon Sugar Syrup
Twist of Lemon Peel

Pour Gin, water and sugar into a chilled old-fashioned glass.

Stir and add an ice cube. Garnish with lemon peel and serve.

H.P.W. Cocktail

31.7% alc/vol

1.5 standard drinks

45ml (1½fl oz) Dry Gin

8ml (¼fl oz) Dry Vermouth

8ml (¼fl oz) Sweet Vermouth

Twist of Orange Peel

Pour Gin and Vermouths into a mixing glass over ice.

Stir and strain into a chilled martini glass.

Garnish with orange peel and serve.

Polo Cocktail No.2

18.3% alc/vol
1.3 standard drinks

45ml (1½fl oz) Gin
23ml (¾fl oz) Grapefruit Juice
23ml (¾fl oz) Fresh Orange Juice

Pour ingredients into a cocktail shaker over ice and shake.

Strain into a chilled cocktail glass and serve.

The Filby

29% alc/vol
1.7 standard drinks

30ml (1fl oz) Dry Gin
15ml (½fl oz) Amaretto
15ml (½fl oz) Campari
15ml (½fl oz) Dry Vermouth
Slice of Orange

Pour Gin, Amaretto, Campari and Vermouth into a mixing glass over ice.

Stir and strain into a chilled cocktail glass.

Garnish with a slice of orange and serve.

Strawberry Fizz

9.9% alc/vol

1.8 standard drinks

60ml (2fl oz) Gin
15ml (½fl oz) Fresh Lemon Juice
15ml (½fl oz) Thick Cream
1 teaspoon Caster Sugar
90ml (3fl oz) Soda Water
4 Strawberries (crushed)
Strawberry

Pour Gin, juice and cream into a cocktail shaker over ice.

Add sugar and crushed strawberries.

Shake and strain into a glass over ice.

Add soda and stir gently.

Garnish with a strawberry and serve.

This drink is also known as Strawberry Blush.

Watermelon Cooler

15.9% alc/vol

1.3 standard drinks

45ml (1½fl oz) Gin

60ml (2fl oz) Watermelon Juice

Pour ingredients into a mixing glass over ice and stir.

Strain into a chilled champagne saucer and serve.

Gin Buck

13.5% alc/vol
1.8 standard drinks

60ml (2fl oz) Gin
½ Fresh Lemon
90ml (3fl oz) Dry Ginger Ale

Pour Gin into a highball glass over ice and twist ½ lemon above drink to release juice then add spent shell.

Stir and add ginger ale. Stir gently and serve.

Gin Daiquiri

27.8% alc/vol

1.8 standard drinks

45ml (1½fl oz) Gin

15ml (½fl oz) Light Rum

15ml (½fl oz) Fresh Lime Juice

1 teaspoon Sugar Syrup

Prepare a cocktail glass with a sugar frosted rim.

Pour ingredients into a cocktail shaker over ice and shake.

Strain into prepared glass and serve.

Harry's

29.8% alc/vol
3.2 standard drinks

90ml (3fl oz) Dry Gin
45ml (1½fl oz) Sweet
Vermouth
Dash Pernod
2 Sprigs of Fresh Mint

Pour Gin, Vermouth, Pernod and a sprig of mint into a cocktail shaker over ice.

Shake and strain into a chilled cocktail glass.

Garnish with a sprig of mint and serve.

Tom Collins

10.3% alc/vol

1.7 standard drinks

60ml (2fl oz) Dry Gin

60ml (2fl oz) Fresh Lemon Juice

1 teaspoon Sugar Syrup

90ml (3fl oz) Soda Water

Maraschino Cherry

Slice of Lemon

Pour Gin, juice and sugar into a glass over ice.

Stir, add soda and stir gently.

Garnish with a cherry and slice of lemon then serve.

Hoffman House Cocktail

30.6% alc/vol
1.6 standard drinks

45ml (1½fl oz) Dry Gin
23ml (¾fl oz) Dry Vermouth
Olive

Pour Gin and Vermouth into a mixing glass over ice.

Stir and strain into a chilled martini glass.

Add an olive and serve.

Gin Sour

28.5% alc/vol

1.8 standard drinks

60ml (2fl oz) Gin

15ml (½fl oz) Fresh Lemon Juice

½ teaspoon Sugar Syrup

Slice of Lemon

Pour Gin, juice and sugar into a cocktail shaker over ice.

Shake and strain into a chilled sour glass.

Garnish with a slice of lemon and serve.

Woodstock

20.1% alc/vol

1.3 standard drinks

45ml (1½fl oz) Dry Gin

Dash Orange Bitters

30ml (1fl oz) Fresh Lemon Juice

1½ teaspoons Maple Syrup

Pour ingredients into a cocktail shaker over ice and shake.

Strain into a chilled cocktail glass and serve.

Wilson Standard

36.6% alc/vol
2.7 standard drinks

90ml (3fl oz) Dry Gin
2 dashes Dry Vermouth
2 Slices of Orange

Pour Gin and Vermouth into a cocktail shaker over ice.

Shake and strain into a chilled cocktail glass.

Garnish with slices of orange and serve.

Singapore Sling

22.9% alc/vol
1.8 standard drinks

45ml (1½fl oz) Gin
23ml (¾fl oz) Cherry Brandy
Dash Angostura Bitters
Dash Bénédictine
30ml (1fl oz) Fresh Lemon Juice
Slice of Orange
Strawberry

Pour Gin, Brandy, Bitters and juice into a cocktail shaker over ice.

Shake and strain into a highball glass filled with ice then layer Bénédicti ne on top.

Garnish with a slice of orange and a strawberry then serve with a straw.

Gin Sling

12.2% alc/vol

1.7 standard drinks

60ml (2fl oz) Gin

Dash Grenadine

30ml (1fl oz) Fresh Orange Juice

90ml (3fl oz) Soda Water

Maraschino Cherry

Slice of Lemon

Pour Gin, Grenadine and juice into a highball glass over ice. Add soda and stir gently.

Garnish with a cherry and slice of lemon then serve.

Long Beach Iced Tea

13.4% alc/vol

2.2 standard drinks

15ml (½fl oz) Gin

15ml (½fl oz) Cointreau

15ml (½fl oz) Gold Tequila

15ml (½fl oz) Light Rum

15ml (½fl oz) Vodka

90ml (3fl oz) Cranberry Juice

30ml (1fl oz) Fresh Lemon Juice

15ml (½fl oz) Sugar Syrup

Slice of Lemon

Pour Gin, Cointreau, Tequila, Rum, Vodka, lemon juice and sugar into a cocktail shaker over ice.

Shake and strain into a highball glass over ice.

Add cranberry juice and stir. Garnish with a slice of lemon and serve.

Captain Cook

22.8% alc/vol

1.6 standard drinks

45ml (1½fl oz) Gin

15ml (½fl oz) Maraschino
Liqueur

30ml (1fl oz) Fresh Orange Juice

Pour ingredients into a cocktail shaker over ice
and shake.

Strain into a chilled cocktail glass and serve.

Strawberry Swig

29.5% alc/vol

1.6 standard drinks

45ml (1½fl oz) Gin

15ml (½fl oz) Strawberry Liqueur

Dash Orange Bitters

8ml (¼fl oz) Fresh Lime Juice

Slice of Lime

Pour Gin, Liqueur, Bitters and juice into a cocktail shaker over ice.

Shake and strain into an old-fashioned glass over ice. Garnish with a slice of lime and serve.

Gin Fizz

12% alc/vol
1.8 standard drinks

60ml (2fl oz) Dry Gin

15ml (½fl oz) Fresh Lemon Juice

15ml (½fl oz) Fresh Lime Juice

1 teaspoon Caster Sugar

White of 1 Egg

60ml (2fl oz) Soda Water

Slice of Lemon

Pour Gin, juices and egg white into a cocktail shaker over ice then add sugar.

Shake and strain into a highball glass over ice.

Add soda and stir gently.

Garnish with a slice of lemon and serve with a straw.

This drink is also known as Silver Fizz.

Sweet Gibson

26% alc/vol

1.8 standard drinks

45ml (1½fl oz) Gin
45ml (1½fl oz) Sweet Vermouth
Cocktail Onion

Pour Gin and Vermouth into a mixing glass over ice. Stir and strain into a chilled cocktail glass.

Add a cocktail onion and serve.

This drink is also known as Gin and it.

Dry Gibson

27.5% alc/vol
2 standard drinks

45ml (1½fl oz) Dry Gin
45ml (1½fl oz) Dry Vermouth
Cocktail Onion

Pour Gin and Vermouth into a mixing glass over ice.

Stir and strain into a chilled cocktail glass.

Garnish with a cocktail onion and serve.

Gentleman's Club

23.9% alc/vol

2.5 standard drinks

45ml (1½fl oz) Gin

30ml (1fl oz) Brandy

30ml (1fl oz) Sweet
Vermouth

30ml (1fl oz) Soda Water

Pour the Gin, Brandy and Vermouth into an old-fashioned glass over ice.

Stir and add soda.

Stir gently and serve.

Yale Cocktail

31.6% alc/vol

1.6 standard drinks

45ml (1½ fl oz) Gin
15ml (½fl oz) Dry Vermouth
5ml (⅙fl oz) Blue Curaçao
Dash Orange Bitters

Pour ingredients into a mixing glass over ice and stir.

Strain into a chilled cocktail glass and serve.

Negroni

28.6% alc/vol

2.7 standard drinks

60ml (2fl oz) Gin

30ml (1fl oz) Campari

30ml (1fl oz) Sweet Vermouth

Slice of Orange

Pour Gin, Campari and Vermouth into a mixing glass over ice.

Stir and strain into a chilled brandy balloon over a few ice cubes.

Top up with soda water if desired and stir gently.

Garnish with a slice of orange and serve.

Negroni - Zimbabwe Style

11.4% alc/vol
0.9 standard drinks

20ml (⅔fl oz) Gin
10ml (⅓fl oz) Campari
10ml (⅓fl oz) Sweet Vermouth
60ml (2fl oz) Fresh Orange Juice

Prepare an old-fashioned glass with a sugar frosted rim and add ice.

Pour ingredients into a cocktail shaker over ice and shake.

Strain into prepared glass and serve.

Negroni No.2

24% alc/vol

1.4 standard drinks

23ml (¾fl oz) Gin

23ml (¾fl oz) Campari

23ml (¾fl oz) Sweet Vermouth

5ml (⅙fl oz) Soda Water

Twist of Lemon Peel

Pour Gin, Campari and Vermouth into a mixing glass over ice.

Stir and strain into a chilled cocktail glass.

Add soda and stir gently.

Garnish with lemon peel and serve.

Gin Mint Fix

24.6% alc/vol

1.8 standard drinks

60ml (2fl oz) Gin
5ml (⅙fl oz) White Crème De Menthe
15ml (½fl oz) Fresh Lemon Juice
10ml (⅓fl oz) Spring Water
1 teaspoon Sugar Syrup
2 Fresh Mint Leaves

Pour Gin, Crème De Menthe, juice, water and sugar into an old-fashioned glass filled with crushed ice.

Add more crushed ice to fill glass and stir.

Float mint leaves on top and serve.

Park Avenue

26.3% alc/vol

1.4 standard drinks

45ml (1½fl oz) Gin
8ml (¼fl oz) Sweet Vermouth
15ml (½fl oz) Pineapple Juice

Pour ingredients into a mixing glass over ice and stir.

Strain into a chilled cocktail glass and serve.

Bloody Martini

27.8% alc/vol

1.4 standard drinks

45ml (1½fl oz) Dry Gin

5ml (⅙fl oz) Dry Vermouth

8ml (¼fl oz) Grenadine

5ml (⅙fl oz) Fresh Lemon Juice

Cherry

Twist of Orange Peel

Pour juice into a frosted martini glass and swirl around glass then discard remainder of juice.

Pour Gin, Vermouth and Grenadine into a cocktail shaker over ice.

Shake and strain into prepared glass.

Garnish with a cherry and orange peel then serve.

London

34.6% alc/vol

1.4 standard drinks

45ml (1½fl oz) Dry Gin

2 dashes Maraschino Liqueur

2 dashes Orange Bitters

2 dashes Sugar Syrup

Twist of Lemon Peel

Pour Gin, Liqueur, Bitters and sugar into a mixing glass over ice.

Stir and strain into a chilled cocktail glass.

Garnish with lemon peel and serve.

Perfect Martini

26.8% alc/vol

1.3 standard drinks

30ml (1fl oz) Dry Gin

15ml (½fl oz) Dry Vermouth

15ml (½fl oz) Sweet Vermouth

Pour ingredients into a mixing glass over ice and stir gently.

Strain into a chilled martini glass and serve.

La Stephanique

33.4% alc/vol

2 standard drinks

45ml (1½fl oz) Gin

15ml (½fl oz) Cointreau

15ml (½fl oz) Sweet
Vermouth

Dash Angostura Bitters

Pour ingredients into a cocktail shaker over ice
and shake.

Strain into a chilled cocktail glass and serve.

Wimbledon Cup

13.8% alc/vol

1.5 standard drinks

30ml (1fl oz) Gin

30ml (1fl oz) Pimm's No.1

30ml (1fl oz) Mandarin Juice

30ml (1fl oz) Thick Cream

15ml (½fl oz) Strawberry Syrup

Pour ingredients into a cocktail shaker over ice and shake.

Strain into a chilled champagne saucer and serve.

Dry Martini

33.8% alc/vol
2.4 standard drinks

75ml (2½fl oz) Dry Gin
15ml (½fl oz) Dry Vermouth
Olive

Pour Gin and Vermouth into a mixing glass over ice.

Stir and strain into a chilled martini glass.

Add an olive and serve.

Sweet Martini

29.7% alc/vol

2.1 standard drinks

60ml (2fl oz) Gin

30ml (1fl oz) Sweet Vermouth

Maraschino Cherry

Pour Gin and Vermouth into a mixing glass over ice.

Stir and strain into a chilled martini glass. Add a cherry and serve.

Smoky Martini

36.5% alc/vol

1.5 standard drinks

50ml (1⅔fl oz) Dry Gin

Dash Dry Vermouth

Dash Scotch Whisky

Pour ingredients into a mixing glass over ice and stir.

Strain into a frosted martini glass and serve.

Gin and Campari

31% alc/vol
1.9 standard drinks

38ml (1¼fl oz) Gin
38ml (1¼fl oz) Campari
Twist of Orange Peel

Pour Gin and Campari into a mixing glass over ice.

Stir and strain into a chilled cocktail glass.

Twist orange peel above drink and place remainder of peel into drink then serve.

Trinity

23.3% alc/vol
1.7 standard drinks

30ml (1fl oz) Dry Gin
30ml (1fl oz) Dry Vermouth
30ml (1fl oz) Sweet Vermouth

Pour ingredients into a mixing glass over ice and stir.

Strain into a chilled cocktail glass and serve.

Knickerbocker Cocktail

30.6% alc/vol

1.6 standard drinks

45ml (1½fl oz) Gin

23ml (¾fl oz) Dry Vermouth

Twist of Lemon Peel

Pour Gin and Vermouth into a mixing glass over ice.

Stir and strain into a chilled cocktail glass.

Add lemon peel and serve.

Dirty Martini

30.6% alc/vol
1.8 standard drinks

60 ml (2 oz) dry gin
10–15 ml (⅓–½ oz) dry vermouth
Add 15 ml (½ fl oz) olive brine
Green Olives

Pour gin and vermouth into a mixing glass

over ice and then add olivebrine then stir until liquid is chilled.

Strain into a chilled martini glass, add olives then serve.

Apertivo Cocktail

36.9% alc/vol

2.3 standard drinks

45ml (1½fl oz) Gin

30ml (1fl oz) Sambuca

3 dashes Orange Bitters

Pour ingredients into a cocktail shaker over ice and shake.

Strain into a chilled cocktail glass and serve.

Hula-Hula Cocktail

30.8% alc/vol

1.3 standard drinks

45ml (1½fl oz) Gin

8ml (¼fl oz) Fresh Orange Juice

Dash Sugar Syrup

Pour ingredients into a cocktail shaker over ice and shake.

Strain into a chilled cocktail glass and serve.

The Jockey Club

31.8% alc/vol

2.2 standard drinks

60ml (2fl oz) Dry Gin

10ml (⅓fl oz) Amaretto

5ml (⅙fl oz) Cointreau

Dash Angostura Bitters

10ml (⅓fl oz) Fresh Lemon Juice

Pour ingredients into a cocktail shaker over ice and shake.

Strain into an old-fashioned glass over ice and serve.

Gin Southern

29.2% alc/vol
1.8 standard drinks

45ml (1½fl oz) Gin
15ml (½fl oz) Southern Comfort
8ml (¼fl oz) Grapefruit Juice
8ml (¼fl oz) Fresh Lemon Juice

Pour ingredients into a cocktail shaker over ice and shake.

Strain into a chilled cocktail glass and serve.

Long Island Iced Tea

22% alc/vol

4 standard drinks

30 ml (1 fl oz) vodka

30 ml (1 fl oz) white rum

30 ml (1 fl oz) Cointreau

30 ml (1 fl oz) tequila

30 ml (1 fl oz) gin

30 ml (1 fl oz) lemon juice

dash of cola

30 ml (1 fl oz) sugar syrup

Pour all ingredients except for cola into a cocktail shaker over ice and shake.

Strain over fresh ice and top with cola.

The tea-coloured cola is splashed into the cocktail making it slightly unsuitable for a "tea party"

Mint Martini

32.4% alc/vol

2.3 standard drinks

60ml (2fl oz) Gin

30ml (1fl oz) Green Crème De Menthe

3 Fresh Mint Leaves

Pour Gin and Crème De Menthe into a mixing glass over ice.

Stir and strain into a chilled martini glass.

Garnish with mint leaves and serve.

Martian Martini

31.7% alc/vol

2.3 standard drinks

60 ml (2 fl oz) gin

30 ml (1 fl oz) Midori

Pour ingredients into a cocktail shaker over ice and shake.

Strain into a chilled martini glass and serve.

Martini Oriental

31.7% alc/vol

1.5 standard drinks

45 ml (1½ fl oz) gin

15 ml (½ fl oz) sake

twist of fresh lemon peel

Pour gin and sake into a mixing glass over ice then stir.

Strain into a chilled martini glass and garnish with a twist of lemon peel then serve.

Paisley Martini

33.7% alc/vol

2.1 standard drinks

60 ml (2 fl oz) gin
15 ml (½ fl oz) dry vermouth
5 ml (⅙ fl oz) scotch whisky
twist of fresh lemon peel

Pour gin, vermouth and whisky into an old-fashioned glass half-filled with ice then stir.

Garnish with a twist of lemon peel and serve.

Gimlet

40% alc/vol

1.5 standard drinks

60 ml (2 fl oz) gin

30 ml (1 fl oz) lime juice

15 ml (½ fl oz) sugar syrup

Pour ingredients into a cocktail shaker. Shake over ice and pour, then add cubed ice.

This cocktail can also be made using pear juice.

Adjust sugar syrup to taste

Gin Toddy

30.4% alc/vol

1.8 standard drinks

60ml (2fl oz) Dry Gin

10ml (⅓fl oz) Spring Water

½ teaspoon Sugar Syrup

Twist of Lemon Peel

Pour Gin, water and sugar into a chilled old-fashioned glass.

Stir and add an ice cube.

Garnish with lemon peel and serve.

Gin Sangaree

14.4% alc/vol
2.5 standard drinks

60ml (2fl oz) Dry Gin

15ml (½fl oz) Port

5ml (⅙ fl oz) Spring Water

½ teaspoon Sugar Syrup

90ml (3fl oz) Soda Water

Nutmeg

Pour Gin, water and sugar into a highball glass over ice.

Add soda and stir gently then layer Port on top.

Sprinkle nutmeg on top and serve.

Greyhound

33% alc/vol
1.8 standard drinks

45ml (1½ fl oz) Dry Gin
150ml (5 fl oz) Grapefruit Juice

Pour Gin into a highball glass over ice and add juice, stir then serve.

Gin Highball

14.8% alc/vol

1.8 standard drinks

60ml (2fl oz) Dry Gin

90ml (3fl oz) Dry Ginger Ale

or Soda Water

Twist of Lemon Peel

Pour Gin into a highball glass over ice and add ginger ale or soda as desired then stir gently.

Garnish with lemon peel and serve.

Pink Gin

37.4% alc/vol
1.9 standard drinks

60ml (2fl oz) Gin
3 dashes Angostura Bitters

Pour Bitters into a chilled goblet and swirl
around glass, then discard remaining Bitters.

Add ice and Gin then serve.

Strawberry Martini

33% alc/vol
1.8 standard drinks

60 ml (2 fl oz) gin
5 ml (⅙ fl oz) dry vermouth
5 ml (⅙ fl oz) grenadine
fresh strawberry

Prepare a martini glass with a sugar frosted rim – moistened with fresh strawberry juice.

Pour gin, vermouth and grenadine into a mixing glass over ice then stir.

Strain into prepared glass and add a strawberry then serve.

Tango Cocktail

22.1% alc/vol
1.4 standard drinks

30ml (1fl oz) Gin
15ml (½fl oz) Dry Vermouth
15ml (½fl oz) Sweet Vermouth
3 dashes Cointreau
15ml (½fl oz) Fresh Orange Juice

Pour ingredients into a cocktail shaker over ice and shake.

Strain into a chilled cocktail glass and serve.

Petticoat Lane

31.4% alc/vol

2.2 standard drinks

60ml (2fl oz) Gin

15ml (½fl oz) Campari

15ml (½fl oz) Sweet Vermouth

Slice of Lemon

Pour Gin, Campari and Vermouth into a mixing glass over ice.

Stir and strain into a chilled cocktail glass.

Garnish with a slice of lemon and serve

Saketini

33.4% alc/vol
2.4 standard drinks

75 ml (2½ fl oz) dry gin
15 ml (½ fl oz) sake
Twist of fresh lemon peel

Pour gin and sake into a mixing glass over ice then stir. Strain

into a chilled martini glass and garnish with a twist of lemon peel then serve.

Golden Daze

22.3% alc/vol

1.6 standard drinks

45ml (1½fl oz) Dry Gin

15ml (½fl oz) Peach Brandy

30ml (1fl oz) Fresh Orange Juice

Pour ingredients into a cocktail shaker over ice and shake.

Strain into a chilled cocktail glass and serve

Orange Blossom

14.8% alc/vol

0.9 standard drinks

30ml (1fl oz) Gin
45ml (1½fl oz) Fresh Orange Juice
Slice of Orange

Pour Gin and juice into a cocktail shaker over ice.

Shake and strain into a chilled cocktail glass.

Garnish with a slice of orange and serve.

Piccadilly Cocktail

30.1% alc/vol
1.7 standard drinks

45ml (1½fl oz) Dry Gin
23ml (¾fl oz) Dry Vermouth
Dash Anisette
Dash Grenadine

Pour ingredients into a mixing glass over ice and stir.

Strain into a chilled cocktail glass and serve.

Income Tax Cocktail

25.5% alc/vol

1.1 standard drinks

30ml (1fl oz) Dry Gin

8ml (¼fl oz) Dry Vermouth

8ml (¼fl oz) Sweet
Vermouth

Dash Orange Bitters

23ml (¾fl oz) Fresh Orange
Juice

Pour ingredients into a cocktail shaker over ice
and shake.

Strain into a chilled cocktail glass and serve.

Gin Sour

28.5% alc/vol

1.8 standard drinks

60ml (2fl oz) Gin

15ml (½fl oz) Fresh Lemon Juice

½ teaspoon Sugar Syrup

Slice of Lemon

Pour Gin, juice and sugar into a cocktail shaker over ice.

Shake and strain into a chilled glass.

Garnish with a slice of lemon and serve.

Bartender

22.5% alc/vol

1.4 standard drinks

20ml (⅔fl oz) Gin

20ml (⅔fl oz) Dry Sherry

20ml (⅔fl oz) Dry Vermouth

20ml (⅔fl oz) Dubonnet

Dash Grand Marnier

Pour ingredients into a mixing glass over ice and stir.

Strain into a chilled cocktail glass and serve.

The Journalist

35.2% alc/vol

1.5 standard drinks

45ml (1½fl oz) Dry Gin

2 dashes Angostura Bitters

2 dashes Cointreau

Dash Dry Vermouth

Dash Sweet Vermouth

2 dashes Fresh Lemon Juice

Pour ingredients into a cocktail shaker over ice and shake.

Strain into a chilled cocktail glass and serve.

Gin and Tonic

12.3% alc/vol
1.3 standard drinks

45ml (1½fl oz) Gin
90ml (3fl oz) Tonic Water
Wedge of Lime

Pour Gin into a glass over ice and twist wedge of lime above drink to release juice.

Stir, add tonic and stir gently.

Add spent lime shell and serve.

Southern Martini

33.3% alc/vol

2.4 standard drinks

60 ml (2 fl oz) gin

15 ml (½ fl oz) Southern Comfort

15 ml (½ fl oz) sweet vermouth

Maraschino cherry

Pour gin, Southern Comfort and vermouth into a mixing glass over ice then stir.

Strain into a chilled martini glass and garnish with a maraschino cherry then serve.

Leaning Tower

35.4% alc/vol

1.9 standard drinks

60ml (2fl oz) Gin
5ml (⅙fl oz) Dry Vermouth
2 dashes Orange Bitters

Pour ingredients into a mixing glass over ice and stir.

Strain into a chilled cocktail glass and serve.

Gin and Bitter-Lemon

9.1% alc/vol
1.3 standard drinks

45ml (1½fl oz) Gin
15ml (½fl oz) Fresh Lemon Juice
½ teaspoon Caster Sugar
120ml (4fl oz) Tonic Water
garnish with mint

Pour Gin, juice and sugar into a cocktail shaker over ice.

Shake and strain into a highball glass over ice.

Add tonic, stir gently and serve.

The Captain's Martini

32.3% alc/vol

1.7 standard drinks

45 ml (1½ fl oz) gin

15 ml (½ fl oz) white crème de menthe

5 ml (⅙ fl oz) dry vermouth

Pour ingredients into a cocktail shaker over ice and shake.

Strain into a chilled martini glass and serve.

Stubby Collins

22.8% alc/vol

1.3 standard drinks

45ml (1½fl oz) Gin

23ml (¾fl oz) Fresh Lemon Juice

1 teaspoon Sugar Syrup

Pour ingredients into a mixing glass over ice and stir.

Strain into a collins glass over ice and serve.

Tidbit

12.4% alc/vol
0.9 standard drinks

30ml (1fl oz) Dry Gin
Dash Dry Sherry
2 scoops Vanilla Ice Cream

Pour ingredients into a blender and blend until smooth.

Pour into a chilled highball glass and serve.

Gilroy

23.3% alc/vol

1.7 standard drinks

30ml (1fl oz) Gin

30ml (1fl oz) Cherry Brandy

15ml (½fl oz) Dry Vermouth

Dash Angostura Bitters

15ml (½fl oz) Fresh Lemon Juice

Maraschino Cherry

Twist of Orange Peel

Pour Gin, Brandy, Vermouth, Bitters and juice into a cocktail shaker over ice.

Shake and strain into a chilled cocktail glass.

Garnish with a cherry and orange peel then serve.

Dunk

33.8% alc/vol
2 standard drinks

45ml (1½fl oz) Dry Gin
15ml (½fl oz) Blue Curaçao
15ml (½fl oz) Galliano
Twist of Orange Peel
Pour Gin, Curaçao and

Galliano into a cocktail shaker over ice.

Shake and strain into a chilled cocktail glass.

Garnish with orange peel and serve.

Passionfruit Cocktail

26.4% alc/vol

2.4 standard drinks

75ml (2½fl oz) Gin

15ml (½fl oz) Dry Vermouth

Pulp of 1 Passionfruit

1 teaspoon Passionfruit

Mint leave for garnish

Pour Gin, Vermouth and pulp of 1 Passionfruit into a mixing glass over ice.

Stir and strain into a chilled cocktail glass.

Add teaspoon of Passionfruit on top and serve.

Flying Dutchman

37% alc/vol
1.8 standard drinks

60ml (2fl oz) Gin
Dash Cointreau

Pour ingredients into a cocktail shaker over ice and shake.

Strain into an old-fashioned glass over ice and serve.

Space

28.8% alc/vol
1.9 standard drinks

45ml (1½fl oz) Gin
30ml (1fl oz) Frangelico
8ml (¼fl oz) Fresh Lemon Juice

Pour ingredients into a cocktail shaker over ice and shake.

Strain into an old-fashioned glass over ice and serve.

Gin Mist

37% alc/vol

1.8 standard drinks

60ml (2fl oz) Gin

Twist of Lime Peel

Pour Gin into an old-fashioned glass over crushed ice and twist lime peel above drink.

Place remainder of peel into drink and serve.

Baron Cocktail

32.7% alc/vol
1.8 standard drinks

45ml (1½fl oz) Gin

15ml (½fl oz) Dry Vermouth

8ml (¼fl oz) Cointreau

2 dashes Sweet Vermouth

Twist of Lemon Peel

Pour Gin, Vermouths and Cointreau into a mixing glass over ice.

Stir and strain into a chilled cocktail glass.

Garnish with lemon peel and serve.

Index

First published in 2022 by New Holland Publishers, Sydney
Level 1, 178 Fox Valley Road, Wahroonga, 2076, NSW, Australia

newhollandpublishers.com

A record of this book is held at the National Library of
Australia

ISBN : 9781760794712

Group Managing Director: Fiona Schultz
Designer: Ben Taylor
Production Director: Arlene Gippert
Printed in China

10 9 8 7 6 5 4 3 2 1

Keep up with New Holland Publishers

f NewHollandPublishers

⚬ @newhollandpublishers